REIGN

Restoring the Process, Pursuit, and Power of Daily Purpose through Prayer

Toni Roberts Sinegal

Every significant moment in
our lives begins in Prayer

"Let us then approach God's throne of grace with confidence so that we may receive mercy and find grace to help us in our time of need."

(Hebrews 4:16)

Dedication

I am extremely grateful for the love, prayers, and prayer requests from others that push me to the place of prayer. Therefore, I dedicate this book to everyone who has ever said or needed prayer. I dedicate this book to those who may have felt like life disqualified them from praying. I dedicate this book to those who know prayer is vital but are unsure where to start.

I dedicate this book to the late Mrs. Lennette Roberts, my grandmother. Growing up, my grandmother (Gram) was a model of faith and trusted in God's Word and prayer. She believed in God when things were impossible, worshipped Him instead of worrying, and filled our home with pockets of prayer throughout the day. Gram would ask the Holy Spirit to lead her to anything, from missing car keys to the miraculous healing of others. I have been told that when I was five years old, she declared I would one day preach the Word of God. Clearly, that was God talking through her because I was something else back then. Nevertheless, she was right.

In 2007, I started preaching. I was blessed for my Gram, the precious oil she carried, and her contagious praise to be present for one year of my ministry. In that year, I benefited from and appreciated the fruit of her relationship with God. I was blessed to call her to pray and when I wanted to know more from God's

Word, as she had committed it to her heart and knew it like the back of her hand.

In July 2008, as God would have it, I was present in the room the day her earthly body expired, and eternity became her home. In between breaths, she reminded me that I belong to God, to do what I needed to ensure Heaven as my home, that Barak Obama would become President, and never to stop praying. As my mother and I stood there while she took her last breath, memories, her teachings, and the mantle of prayer filled my heart and spirit. I'm not sure if this is a dedication as much as it is an immense appreciation for the woman God used to pass down a tenacious desire for His Word, real ministry through loving others, and a heart posture of prayer that evokes the presence of God. Her spirit is forever in my heart and pushes me to pray. I love you, Gram.

Foreword

REIGN is symbolic of the Genesis and Revelation of Minister Toni Roberts-Sinegal, from the beginning of her life in her mother's womb to life situations that expose her heart's posture as one of prayer. Minister Sinegal has been chosen to carry a mantle of prayer. Through REIGN, Sinegal takes readers on a practical and potent journey of a greater understanding of the power and significance of prayer as an open line of communication with God. As a friend and destiny partner of Toni's, I have not only witnessed her pray with and for others, but I have also experienced the manifestation of healing and deliverance because of her faith through prayer. She not only carries the mantle of prayer, but she also has the spirit of prayer, the spirit to seek His face and enter His presence carrying the woes, worries, and wounds of others without reservation or hesitation, and with an unyielding sacrifice. Her journey of releasing REIGN into the earth comes with years of warring and carrying others to the throne of grace.

As a prayer general, intercessor, and teacher, Minister Sinegal composes her prayer strategies, spiritual and practical, for anyone who desires to pray, intensify their prayer life, or learn more about the power and posture of prayer to do so without delay. REIGN not only helps to restore our prayer life, but it also propels us to a life of prayer. It is a prayer portal designed to elevate our prayer language and awaken the spirit of prayer within us. We were created to REIGN, and Minister Sinegal teaches us how to restore the process, pursuit, and power of our daily purpose through prayer.

Dr. Kimberly Ellison

Corporate Jewel Professional Women

Founder & Vessel

Table of Contents

Preface

As a child, young woman, and an adult, I was guilty of searching for a place of security and identity. In this pursuit, my spirit always led me to the privileged place of God's presence through prayer. No matter the search, feeling, or uncertainty, validation and peace found in prayer solidify that I belong to Him. I wrote this book because everyday life can be difficult. Between self-pressure to social media pressure, there is an intensified need to belong. I wrote this book because prayer was in me before I was into it. I want you to experience daily power, identity, security, reassurance, and restoration in God's presence through prayer. Be it short or long, your prayers are meaningful for you and others. In God's presence through prayer, we find who we are, what we need, and most importantly, we find God. The greatest gift prayer yields is God's presence. I believe in the power of prayer and want you to experience it daily.

Introduction

All too often, prayer is passed off as something old or boring. However, prayer is not a thing; it is a place. Secondly, once we understand it, prayer is far from boring. Some don't bother with praying because they feel disconnected or unqualified or have experienced life in a way that makes prayer seem ineffective. Prayer through God's Word causes us to *Reign* over what once rained on us. I want those who find prayer familiar or foreign to be restored through knowledge of prayer. I want those who know that we cannot do life on our own to become comfortable with prayer. I want women to be restored through the place of prayer in God's presence, knowing that what we take to Him, He handles. Whether your prayer is as simple as "Jesus wept," a long dialogue, a silent moment, sighs, tears, tantrums, on the go, or in a set place, God is near when we sincerely reach out to Him. Do not stop praying. There is power for daily purpose in prayer!

The Purpose, Process, and Promises of Prayer

It would be beneficial to be briefed on what I like to refer to as the what, why, and how of prayer. Those components are a bundle of understanding of what we are doing, and the why and how provide longevity beyond the surface. I want you to know that prayer is not assigned to one individual. I am not saying that certain people do not have a mantle to pray in-depth, but I am saying that we can and should pray. The Bible says it this way: "Then Jesus told his disciples a parable to show them that they should always pray and not give up" (Luke 18:1).

You might be wondering why we pray or what prayer has to do with reigning in every area of your purpose.

Let's go back to the basics to build a substantial foundation. Beyond repetition or religious rhetoric, God is calling us to a place of prayer. We live in a day in which we and the world around us have several questions, and the root of any response begins in prayer. Those questions can better be evaluated and answered by a broadened understanding of prayer.

In the old days, the church would refer to prayer as "a little talk with Jesus."

I like that.

Prayer is, in part, a talk with Jesus ("in part" because prayer is not just composed of us talking). I have heard many definitions of prayer, but I will provide my meaning: Prayer is communicating with God via words, sounds, tears, thoughts, and listening.

I wanted to make sure I included listening as a form of prayer. I mean, how rude is it to spill and speak to someone and not wait to see if they wish to respond? When we pray and pause, it shows we care about God's guidance on what we presented to Him. Prayer is a language between Earth and Heaven that has no limits on distance because it is spiritual. Prayer goes where we do not have access and does what we do not have the authority to do. Prayer invites God to be a part of our lives and intervene in our daily lives, and it is a weapon against the tricks of the enemy and our feelings. Prayer is a form of communication with God that edifies and builds our spirit to increases our faith. For so long, prayer has been referred to as a thing we do, but prayer is a place we go.

I am forever grateful for my mama, who still stirs me in prayer when I visit home. Throughout the years, the sound of prayer, worship, and travail would come from her prayer closet and change the atmosphere. To have a mama who prays for you, before you, and for others created my foundation and my sisters' foundation, too. I am grateful that somebody prayed for me.

Our prayers should be intentional and strategic. If we wanted someone to give us a gourmet meal, we wouldn't ask for fingernail polish. The two have nothing to do with each other. We must have the same mindset about prayer. If we pray in faith, we should be direct and clear, confident not in ourselves but in our God, who responds to our prayers. When we pray intentionally, we are saying that we trust God with every detail. One of the sincerest and most rewarding gifts to ourselves and others is prayer.

We pray in faith and according to God's Will.

Faith is a belief and conviction. Faith is confidence in what we hope for and the assurance that the Lord is working, even though we cannot see it. Faith knows that no matter the situation in our lives or someone else's life, the Lord is working. The Bible speaks of and encourages us in our faith. You will pray to Him, and He will hear you, and you will fulfill your vows (Job 22:27): "Now faith is confidence in what we hope for and assurance about what we do not see" (Hebrew 11:1). "Let us then approach God's throne of grace with confidence, so that we may receive mercy and find grace to help us in our time of need" (Hebrews 4:16).

Another great reason to pray confidently is that Jesus Christ is our mediator and spokesperson. He speaks on our behalf when we pray to God the Father. Jesus is sitting at the right hand of the Father, intentionally standing in the gap for us. When we pray, we are in a place of exchange. We take our problems to Jesus, and in exchange, He gives them to God on our behalf: "'Look,'" he said, 'I see heaven open and the Son of Man standing at the right hand of God'" (Acts 7:56).

Now we know what prayer is and a few reasons why we should pray. Prayer is not always about the outcome as it is the inner work. Prayer ignites our relationship with God. Prayer is a place of intimacy, and through our prayer time with God, our trust in Him builds. Like anyone we choose to spend time with, prayer causes us to know God more. The more we know about God, the more confident we are in His ability.

See, praying is really for us!

In the Bible, Jesus gives us the Lord's Prayer as a model to pray:

Our Father in Heaven, hallowed be your name. Your kingdom come, your Will be done, on Earth as it is in Heaven. Give us today our daily bread. And forgive us our debts, as we also have forgiven our debtors. And lead us not into temptation but deliver us from the evil one (Matthew 6:9-14).

Contrary to what some may think, we do not have to be the most well-versed to pray. Prayer is more about our heart's posture than our vocabulary. Prayer requires no intellect but a heart and spirit that seek Him: "And he who searches our hearts knows the mind of the Spirit because the Spirit intercedes for God's people in accordance with the will of God" (Romans 8:27).

When we pray, we pray inclusive of or founded on God's Word. God responds to what He has already spoken to fulfill it: "For no word from God will ever fail" (Luke 1:37).

If we spend time seeking God, His Will transforms our desires. In prayer, what we think we want is transformed by God's Will for us. Prayer is not just about our situation changing but about how we see it changing. Prayer relinquishes human logic and allows us to trust God's Will, plan, and love for us.

This is the confidence we have in approaching God, that if we ask anything according to His Will, He hears us. And if we know that He hears us—whatever we ask—we know that we have what we asked of Him (1 John 5:14-15).

Prayer is often referred to as a thing we do. I respectfully disagree. Prayer is a place we go. And in that place, we exchange what is heavy or hard for what is light and free. In the place of prayer, we receive the grace that makes hard things possible, and our faith is increased. Be it a few seconds or hours when we pray, we lose ourselves and find Christ. Prayer is a place of empowerment and love. Prayer is not a jerk reaction; it is a proactive posture. Prayer goes before us. We never have to pray. Instead, we are privileged to pray!

When we go to God in prayer and sincerely call on Him, He is near. God wants to hear from us by way of prayer. God promises to listen and, in one way or another, respond when we pray. "Because he turned his ear to me, I will call on him as long as I live" (Psalm 116:2).

No matter what we face, there is a Scripture to incorporate with our prayer. I will provide separate prayers and Scriptures that will serve as a reminder and refuge on days you cannot see your *Reign*. I also have a few examples of topics paired with Scripture. These are things we may feel, need, or seek from God. If we are going to *Reign*, we must have prayer and God's Word.

Resolve How I Feel = Become Restored through Scripture

If you feel anxiety: *"From the ends of the earth, I call to you, I call as my heart grows faint; lead me to the rock that is higher than I"* (Psalm 61:2).

If you feel grief: *"Blessed are those who mourn, for they will be comforted"* (Matthew 5:4).

If you seek wisdom: *"If any of you lacks wisdom, you should ask God, who gives generously to all without finding fault, and it will be given to you"* (James 1:5).

If you feel fear: *"For the Spirit God gave us does not make us timid, but gives us power, love, and self-discipline"* (2 Timothy 1:7).

To tap into love: *"For God so loved the world that he gave his one and only Son, that whoever believes in him shall not perish but have eternal life"* (John 3:16).

For provision: *"And my God will meet all your needs according to the riches of his glory in Christ Jesus"* (Philippians 4:19).

When praying for healing: *"'But I will restore you to health and heal your wounds,' declares the Lord..."* (Jeremiah 30:17).

When praying about your purpose: *"'For I know the plans I have for you,' declares the Lord, 'plans to prosper you and not to harm you, plans to give you hope and a future'"* (Jeremiah 29:11).

People can say what they want, but God's Word is our greatest form of self-help. We were created to *Reign*, but there is no secret sauce. Battles and victories are fought and won in prayer. When we are positioned in prayer daily, we are positioned to *Reign*. Do not stop praying. There is power there: "Call to me, and I will answer you and tell you great and unsearchable things you do not know" (Jeremiah 33:3).

What emotions or feelings am I experiencing?

_____

_____

_____

_____

_____

_____

_____

_____

_____

Scriptures to pray regarding my emotions and feelings:

_____

_____

_____

_____

_____

_____

_____

_____

What emotions or feelings am I experiencing?

_____

_____

_____

_____

_____

_____

_____

_____

Scriptures to pray regarding my emotions and feelings:

_____

_____

_____

_____

_____

_____

_____

_____

_____

What I need from God…

_____

_____

_____

_____

_____

_____

_____

_____

_____

Scriptures to incorporate in prayer regarding my need(s):

_____

_____

_____

_____

_____

_____

_____

_____

What I need from God…

_____

_____

_____

_____

_____

_____

_____

_____

Scriptures to incorporate in prayer regarding my need(s):

_____

_____

_____

_____

_____

_____

_____

_____

_____

I am seeking God for…

_____

_____

_____

_____

_____

_____

_____

_____

Scriptures to pray in alignment with what I am seeking:

_____

_____

_____

_____

_____

_____

_____

_____

_____

I am seeking God for…

_____

_____

_____

_____

_____

_____

_____

_____

Scriptures to pray in alignment with what I am seeking:

_____

_____

_____

_____

_____

_____

_____

_____

What do I hear God saying during prayer?

What do I hear God saying during prayer?

_____

_____

_____

_____

_____

_____

_____

_____

_____

_____

_____

_____

_____

_____

_____

_____

_____

What do I hear God saying during prayer?

What do I hear God saying during prayer?

_____

_____

_____

_____

_____

_____

_____

_____

_____

_____

_____

_____

_____

_____

_____

_____

_____

_____

_____

_____

The Power of Prayer

Prayer is a powerful weapon against the daily battles of life. The late trailblazer Kathryn Kuhlman once said, "The greatest power given to men and women is prayer!" The most powerful and intimate postures of prayer are not captured on camera or heard on a microphone but resonate loudly in Heaven. Prayer changes our perspective. Power is strength, ability, influence, and authority.

Reign Daily Through Prayer

God, I thank You for the privilege of direct access to Your throne by way of prayer. Help me to never take this place with You for granted. There is no pressure in this place, and I receive a supernatural exchange. In Jesus' name, Amen.

God, I thank You that what You will do through me, for me, and in me will be established in prayer. In Jesus' name, Amen.

God, I thank You for Your Word that backs all Your plans and promises for my life. Send Your Word that heals, delivers, frees, and establishes my life. In Jesus' name, Amen.

God, I thank You for being intentional about my life. If I am experiencing trouble, then that trouble has a purpose. In Jesus' name, Amen.

God, thank You for Your presence. In Your presence, I am renewed, refreshed, restored, and redirected. In Your presence, I exchange my gloom for Your glory, my tears for Your joy, and my lack for Your surplus. In Jesus' name, Amen.

God, I come to You in prayer for guidance. I ask that You plant my feet where You have called me, give me focus to set my sights on You, and anoint me to suffer with You so that I may Reign with You. In Jesus' name, Amen.

By the authority of Jesus Christ, we dismantle and dismiss the enemy's plans in our families, homes, and lives. In Jesus' name, Amen.

God, I thank You that Your promises are "yes" and "Amen." Your delay is not denial but preparation for Your promises in my life. In Jesus' name, Amen.

Father God, please open our eyes and show us when we have chosen wrong over right. Help us to serve You and trust You to guide us. We dismiss our egos and are open to Your way. Thank You for giving us opportunities to make our wrongs right. In Jesus' name, Amen.

God, I thank You for warring angels that go before us daily. Before we open our eyes to know what the day will bring, You have dispatched angelic hosts for purposes of protection, provision, and a predetermined outcome. In Jesus' name, Amen.

God, I pray today that You will forgive us for everything we intentionally or unknowingly put before You. Forgive us when we are careless with what and who You give us in this world. Forgive us when we are prideful. Please forgive us for allowing life to make us forget your love, grace, mercy, and faithfulness. In Jesus' name, Amen.

I pray today for those grieving. I pray they are allowed to grieve without being consumed by grief. I speak Your comfort to all who need it. In Jesus' name, Amen.

God, today I come to You with a thankful heart. I focus on Your goodness in my life, and I partner with the angels to give You thanks. I partner with Your creation to praise You. I am thankful for You. In Jesus' name, Amen.

Father God, as a daughter of the King, I thank You that I am uniquely and authentically created in Your image. I pray that I am not moved by the influence of artificial things or people but embrace who I am in You. In Jesus' name, Amen.

God, I ask that the Holy Spirit leads me and that I will be receptive to any whisper or sign I should follow. I acknowledge that I need Your direction and am open to being led. In Jesus' name, Amen.

God, I ask that You help control my voice and emotions so that they do not become too loud for me to hear and sense Your voice. In Jesus' name, Amen.

Today, I pray for protection for dangers seen and unseen. I pray for the spirit of God to go where I cannot go and do what I cannot do. Thank You for everything You saved me from and everything, seen and unseen. In Jesus' name, Amen.

God, I denounce every spirit that tries to attach itself to me to hinder Your moves in my life. I pray that You fight what feels like physical problems but are spiritual battles. In Jesus' name, Amen.

I approach today and its uncertainties, not knowing what today holds but having full faith and confidence in my God, who holds the day. In Jesus' name, Amen.

I speak to every blessing that has my name on it but has been held up. I call forward a release in the natural and in the spirit. I pray that everything that belongs to me would be mine now. In Jesus' name, Amen.

As a believer, I do not pray for victory but from a place of victory. I declare and decree that the enemy I see today I will see no more. In Jesus' name, Amen.

God, today, I ask for increased faith in You. Please forgive me when I do not completely trust what You have spoken. According to Your Word, I believe You have not given me a spirit of fear but of power, love, and a sound mind. I fully walk in it today. In Jesus' name, Amen.

I am enough. I am loved. I am valued. I am thought of by the King of Kings. So today, I pray not to be defined by the labels of the world but to wear the love of Christ that defines me. In Jesus' name, Amen.

I declare and decree that my existence is a byproduct of the plan of God. I am not an accident or a mistake. I pray that my life produces God's full intent. In Jesus' name, Amen.

I pray against spiritual battles that disguise themselves as physical fatigue. The enemy knows that God has great plans for me, so he tries to tire me before I get to the blessing. I declare that I am not tired. I am restored through prayer and have victory in Christ. In Jesus' name, Amen.

Today, I pray for my surroundings. I declare and decree that every environment and atmosphere are subject to the spirit of God. Everything around me is regulated by Christ. In Jesus' name, Amen.

God, today, I thank You for Your presence. Living in a day and time when everyone is searching for a place to belong, I am grateful for my reserved place at Your feet in prayer. In Jesus' name, Amen.

God, today, I pray against car incidents and accidents. I pray that You keep every car in its lane and fatalities will not occur. In Jesus' name, Amen.

Today, I pray for the heart and innocence of children. Children are gifts from You and are covered and protected by You. May every parent, caregiver, relative, and teacher be a part of Your plan to protect our children. In Jesus' name, Amen.

God, today, I come to You with my options and choices. I ask that You make the right choice easy and the wrong one impossible. In Jesus' name, Amen.

God, today, I dismiss the lie that if I am confident, I am arrogant. I accept the Godfidence you have given me and gracefully walk in it. I am sure and secure that I am a masterpiece in You. In Jesus' name, Amen.

God, today, I pray the faults and sins of my past be eradicated. I pray from a heart of repentance and with a clear conscience. I accept Your forgiveness and release my past. In Jesus' name, Amen.

God, today, I lift my family to You. I pray that the blood of Jesus would cancel every bloodline curse. I pray that we are transfused by the blood of Jesus and receive a generational blessing. In Jesus' name, Amen.

God, today, I admit that I am upset. I am asking You to help me with my anger, but sin not. In Jesus' name, Amen.

God, today, I rededicate my life to You. I pray that You cleanse me of all unrighteousness and restore my covenant in Christ. In Jesus' name, Amen.

Today, I pray for a flow of creativity. I pray for fresh vision and ideas. I pray to be positioned as a canvas for the creation of You through me. In Jesus' name, Amen.

Today, I speak my need for more of You. I often feel like I need more money, things, or people, but I really need more of You. In Jesus' name, Amen.

God, I thank You that there is nothing You have assigned to my hands that I am incapable of in Your strength. I relinquish my need to be in control. I ask that You give me what I need for everything You have assigned to me on this day. In Jesus' name, Amen.

God, I take my eyes off my problems and those of this world. I look to You, the Problem Solver. In Jesus' name, Amen.

God, today, I pray that failure is not an option. I will not fail myself, those who are counting on me, or You. Let any letdown, change in plans, or commitments be an opportunity to learn, grow, and trust You more. In Jesus' name, Amen.

God, because of You, I will not run from difficulties or opposition. I declare they are opportunities in disguise. In Jesus' name, Amen.

God, I pray that I will not be intimidated by the timelines of this world. I operate in You and on Your time. I will not run out of time because I run to You first. In Jesus' name, Amen.

God, I dedicate my plans to You. I give You permission to alter and erase anything outside of Your plans. I commit to doing life Your way. In Jesus' name, Amen.

Today, I pray for favor that is uncommon and appears unfair. Thank You in advance for closer parking spots, unexpected money, a favor phone call, a promotion, and every way You break protocol to grant me favor. In Jesus' name, Amen.

God, I pray for the female body and its reproduction system. I pray specifically for those with issues and abnormalities, from irregular periods to unexplainable tumors and everything between and beyond. I pray for the female reproductive system to be preserved. I pray Your blood causes our bodies to line up and regulate. In Jesus' name, Amen.

Today, I pray for my mind. I pray against the battles of my thoughts. I command my mind to line up with the mind of Christ. The mind of Christ says I am whole, restored, stable, and capable. In Jesus' name, Amen.

God, I pray that You would bless me with covenant connections and cause me to be one for others. I pray You to cut the ties of any relationship that destroys my destiny or causes me to destroy the destiny of others. In Jesus' name, Amen.

Today, I pray that I am not too lazy to do the work. For every request I bring to You, please show me my part. I partner with You and expect to be a participant in my manifestation of prayers. In Jesus' name, Amen.

God, I pray for the perseverance to endure the process of Your promises in my life. In Jesus' name, Amen.

Today, I pray for my enemies so that forgiveness may be well with my soul. In Jesus' name, Amen.

God, I ask for the discipline to govern everything You would entrust to me. I pray for the ability to deny my flesh in any way it would mishandle what You give me. From my heart to my body to my mind to my money, I pray for the discipline to manage my manna well. In Jesus' name, Amen.

God, I pray for the courage to love in a way that reflects You. Heal me from every hurt and show me how to give Your love to others. In Jesus' name, Amen.

God, teach me to decipher the difference between good ideas and God ideas. I know that Your plan is perfect and greater. In Jesus' name, Amen.

God, I admit that I do not know what the fight and struggles are all about in my life. I ask that You grant me the tenacity to bring my issues to You repeatedly. There is nothing hidden from You, not a struggle above You. Thank You for a safe place for what I do not understand. In Jesus' name, Amen.

I pray today for the peace of God that goes beyond all human understanding. I pray that amid storms, I, too, will experience Your peace. I pray that You speak to the wind and cause every storm to pass. Thank You for carrying me through the storm and keeping me in peace. In Jesus' name, Amen.

I will not search outside of me for what You have put in me. God, I pray to see the hidden treasure within. In Jesus' name, Amen.

Father God, there is life in You. When I am short of breath and the days knock the wind out of me, I come to You in prayer for Your breath of life. In Jesus' name, Amen.

God, there is no way I can bless You in the ways You have blessed me. I bless You through my praise. I praise You because You are God, and besides You, there is none other. In Jesus' name, Amen.

God, today, I believe You to make crooked places straight, old things new, and the impossible possible. In Jesus' name, Amen.

I pray against the spirit of stagnation that makes us sad, stale, and stuck. I pray for freedom to flow to our purpose. In Jesus' name, Amen.

God, I thank You that prayers are stored up for me when I am too tired or weak. Let the prayers I have previously prayed and those spoken on my behalf stand in the gap for me. In Jesus' name, Amen.

I pray the power of God to dry up sickness and disease. May those who are sick receive healing and the doctor's report be canceled by the report of the Lord and healed in Jesus' name. In Jesus' name, Amen.

God, we know that where You have planted a promise in our lives, the enemy will try to present an imposter. Please help us to discern the difference between real and fake for the sake of our destiny. In Jesus' name, Amen.

God, today I declare that I will be prayerful and not petty. Prayer speaks to situations far better than an immature response. Let us pray. In Jesus' name, Amen.

I command our day and lives to line up with God's Will. We accept angelic hosts to war on our behalf. We speak God's Word of protection, provision, and preparation to establish our day. In Jesus' name, Amen.

I declare and decree that I submit and surrender to God's Will. I will experience the supernatural Will of God, and the Heavens will back up the work of my hands. In Jesus' name, Amen.

God, thank You that a disconnection from daily sources like our job, talents, or money is not a disconnection from You, our ultimate Resource. In Jesus' name, Amen.

Today, I pray for the spirit of revival to break out in me. I pray to be a conduit for Your power and presence. In Jesus' name, Amen.

God, I believe in healing. You sent Your Word and healed them. I pray by the stripes of Jesus Christ that myself and others who are sick would receive healing. In Jesus' name, Amen.

Father God, I thank You for a new day filled with new mercies. I do not ask that You make today like a previous day, but I look for something new and fresh. In Jesus' name, Amen.

Today, I pray that just as Jesus died for our sins, You are granting great exchanges. May our flesh be crucified, and we take on the nature and fruit of You. In Jesus' name, Amen.

God, I thank You for a place to fit in through prayer. I know that when I come to You, it is a setup to receive all that I need and more. In Jesus' name, Amen.

Today, I pray for those who are without. I pray You to bless my hands to bless others. I lift those in bad weather conditions by force or choice and pray for Your shelter. In Jesus' name, Amen.

God, I am grateful for Your resume of overcoming trouble. Because of Your history, I know You are able. In Jesus' name, Amen.

God, I dismiss feelings that would make me silent when I should speak. My words shape my world. I will speak up and of Your Word until I see a manifestation of it. In Jesus' name, Amen.

God, we are faced with so much within a day. I pray for peace. I pray for a renewed faith. Help me not to panic when I should pray. In Jesus' name, Amen.

I pray that I will not merely exist but have an abundant life. In Jesus' name, Amen.

God, I pray that You disrupt, disconnect, and dismantle any relationships in my life that interfere with my destiny. In Jesus' name, Amen.

God, today, I pray that You would lead, and I would follow. In Jesus' name, Amen.

God, I pray that the glass ceiling of regular, ordinary, and mundane be shattered. I was created to live an extraordinary life, outside the box of ordinary. In Jesus' name, Amen.

God, I thank You because the first words of my day are in prayer, and You always speak the last word for me. In Jesus' name, Amen.

God, I thank You that even when You do not move the mountains in my life, You give me the strength to climb them. In Jesus' name, Amen.

Today, I declare that God remembers and answers my prayers from long ago. In Jesus' name, Amen.

Father God, I pray to be consumed by You when life attempts to consume me. Wrap me in Your arms and let Your Word become my greatest reality. In Jesus' name, Amen.

God, thank You that there is a place in prayer that heals, reveals, and conceals. Before I worry about it, I choose to pray about it. In Jesus' name, Amen.

God, I pray today that the root of every negative word curse over my life be destroyed. I speak words of life, prosperity, and freedom to cancel them out. In Jesus' name, Amen.

God, I know that You can restore, redeem, and renew what seems to be years of lost time in just one moment. I thank You for a moment that makes up for a lifetime. In Jesus' name, Amen.

God, Your peace and power proceed us, and Your grace and mercy follow me. It is well in You. In Jesus' name, Amen.

God, I commit all those I love and care for to You. I know that they do not belong to me but You, and I trust You to take care of them. In Jesus' name, Amen.

God, thank You that when I pray sincerely, there is a sound released that summons the angels and scares the enemy. When I pray from my heart and according to Your Will, Heaven hears and helps me. In Jesus' name, Amen.

God, I pray today that the why of my life be revealed. Through pain or gain, I am open to Your purpose and perfect Will for my life. In Jesus' name, Amen.

God, I thank You that in prayer, the ill will of the enemy is interrupted. You change the narrative of our stories. In Jesus' name, Amen.

God, I thank You for the power of prayer that reveals itself in private for what You will do publicly. In Jesus' name, Amen.

Write Your Prayers of Declaration Below.

Example: God, today I declare that I will be prayerful and not petty. Prayer speaks to situations far better than an immature response. Let us pray. In Jesus' name, Amen.

_____

_____

_____

_____

_____

_____

_____

_____

_____

_____

_____

_____

_____

_____

_____

_____

_____

Write Your Prayers of Declaration Below.

Example: *God, today I declare that I will be prayerful and not petty. Prayer speaks to situations far better than an immature response. Let us pray. In Jesus' name, Amen.*

_____

_____

_____

_____

_____

_____

_____

_____

_____

_____

_____

_____

_____

_____

_____

_____

_____

_____

Write Your Prayers of Thanksgiving Below.

Example: God, I thank You that even when You do not move the mountains in my life, You give me the strength to climb them. In Jesus' name, Amen.

_____

_____

_____

_____

_____

_____

_____

_____

_____

_____

_____

_____

_____

_____

_____

_____

_____

_____

_____

Write Your Prayers of Thanksgiving Below.

Example: God, I thank You that even when You do not move the mountains in my life, You give me the strength to climb them. In Jesus' name, Amen.

_____

_____

_____

_____

_____

_____

_____

_____

_____

_____

_____

_____

_____

_____

_____

_____

_____

_____

_____

_____

Write Your Prayers of Protection Below.

Example: Today, I pray for protection for dangers seen and unseen. I pray for the spirit of God to go where I cannot go and do what I cannot do. Thank You for everything You saved me from and everything seen and unseen. In Jesus' name, Amen.

_____

_____

_____

_____

_____

_____

_____

_____

_____

_____

_____

_____

_____

_____

_____

_____

_____

Write Your Prayers of Protection Below.

Example: Today, I pray for protection for dangers seen and unseen. I pray for the spirit of God to go where I cannot go and do what I cannot do. Thank You for everything You saved me from and everything seen and unseen. In Jesus' name, Amen.

_____

_____

_____

_____

_____

_____

_____

_____

_____

_____

_____

_____

_____

_____

_____

_____

_____

_____

Reign in Scripture

God responds to His Word. In addition to prayer, speaking God's Word causes us to *Reign*. Praying according to Scripture benefits us because He fulfills His Word. When we pray the Word of God, we are obligating God to do what He said. And that is His good pleasure. Prayer and Scripture go hand in hand. Prayers are our feeling or expression, and Scripture is God's truth. God can not lie. His Word is without flaw or failure. I look at Scripture as a foundation for prayer. When we do not fully know what to pray, the Holy Spirit and God's holy Word are examples to guide and speak for us. Praying Scriptures prepares our hearts to be open and connected with God to speak to, through, and for us:

So shall my word be that goeth forth out of my mouth: it shall not return unto me void, but it shall accomplish that which I please, and it shall prosper in the thing whereto I sent it (Isaiah 55:11).

"And he that searcheth the hearts knoweth what is the mind of the Spirit because he maketh intercession for the saints according to the will of God" (Romans 8:27).

We don't have to know hundreds of Scriptures by memory, but we can start by remembering our favorites. Be it from the first book of the Bible in Genesis, "In the beginning, God created the Heavens and the Earth," to the last in Revelations that say, "The grace of the Lord Jesus be with God's people" and everything in between, the Word of God works. Thankfully, we have access via the Holy Bible or by computer to God's Word. "Thy word have I hid in mine heart, that I might not sin against thee" (Psalm 119:11).

Sometimes the approach to prayer may seem overwhelming, but Scripture helps calm us and center our focus. No matter the prayer topic, there is relief and a solution found in Scripture. God's Word is His seal and personal guarantee for all who believe. Throughout the Bible, Scripture reveals the who of God. When we pray Scripture, we are praying to God and His fullness. God's Word is Him. The Bible is the living Word and cannot be separated from prayer: "In the beginning was the Word, and the Word was with God, and the Word was God" (John 1:1).

Scriptures for Daily Prayer, Reflection, and Victory

"For no word from God will ever fail."
(Luke 1:37)

"Now to him who is able to do immeasurably more than all we ask or imagine, according to his power that is at work within us."
(Ephesians 3:20)

"In the beginning was the Word, and the Word was with God, and the Word was God."
(John 1:1)

"All Scripture is God-breathed and is useful for teaching, rebuking, correcting, and training in righteousness."
(2 Timothy 3:16)

"My comfort in my suffering is this: Your promise preserves my life."
(Psalm 119:50)

"Teach me your way, Lord, that I may rely on your faithfulness; give me an undivided heart, that I may fear your name."

(Psalm 86:11)

"You will keep in perfect peace those whose minds are steadfast because they trust in you."

(Isaiah 26:3)

"But as for me, I watch in hope for the Lord; I wait for God my Savior; my God will hear me."

(Micah 7:7)

"The Lord bless you and keep you; the Lord make his face shine on you and be gracious to you; the Lord turn his face toward you and give you peace."

(Numbers 6:24-26)

"Set your minds on things above, not on earthly things."

(Colossians 3:2)

"If you say, 'The Lord is my refuge,' and you make the Most High your dwelling, no harm will overtake you, no disaster will come near your tent, for he will command his angels concerning you to guard you in all your ways.'"

(Psalm 91:9-11)

"Nevertheless, I will bring health and healing to it; I will heal my people and will let them enjoy abundant peace and security."
(Jeremiah 33:6)

"He said, 'If you listen carefully to the Lord your God and do what is right in his eyes, if you pay attention to his commands and keep all his decrees, I will not bring on you any of the diseases I brought on the Egyptians, for I am the Lord who heals you.'"
(Exodus 15:26)

"I consider that our present sufferings are not worth comparing with the glory that will be revealed in us."
(Romans 8:18)

"In him, our hearts rejoice, for we trust in his holy name."
(Psalm 33:21)

"The fear of the Lord is the beginning of wisdom; all who follow his precepts have good understanding. To him belongs eternal praise."
(Psalm 111:10)

"You, God, are my God, earnestly I seek you; I thirst for you, my whole being longs for you, in a dry and parched land where there is no water."

(Psalm 63:1)

"Cast your cares on the Lord, and he will sustain you; he will never let the righteous be shaken."

(Psalm 55:22)

"Let the morning bring me word of your unfailing love, for I have put my trust in you. Show me the way I should go, for to you I entrust my life."

(Psalm 143:8)

"Blessed are those who hunger and thirst for righteousness, for they will be filled."

(Matthew 5:6)

"I will instruct you and teach you in the way you should go; I will counsel you with my loving eye on you."

(Psalm 32:8)

"You will keep in perfect peace those whose minds are steadfast because they trust in you."

(Isaiah 26:3)

"Therefore, do not worry about tomorrow, for tomorrow will worry about itself. Each day has enough trouble of its own."
(Matthew 6:34)

"But we have this treasure in jars of clay to show that this all-surpassing power is from God and not from us. We are hard-pressed on every side, but not crushed; perplexed, but not in despair; persecuted, but not abandoned; struck down, but not destroyed."
(2 Corinthians 4:7-9)

"My comfort in my suffering is this: Your promise preserves my life."
(Psalm 119:50)

"God is spirit, and his worshipers must worship in the Spirit and in truth."
(John 4:24)

"With long life, I will satisfy him and show him my salvation."
(Psalm 91:16)

"The Lord will vindicate me; your love, Lord, endures forever—do not abandon the works of your hands."
(Psalm 138:8)

"Now to him who is able to do immeasurably more than all we ask or imagine, according to his power that is at work within us."
(Ephesians 3:20)

"I will come and proclaim your mighty acts, Sovereign Lord; I will proclaim your righteous deeds, yours alone."
(Psalm 71:16)

"Before I formed you in the womb, I knew you; before you were born, I set you apart; I appointed you as a prophet to the nations."
(Jeremiah 1:5)

"For where your treasure is, there your heart will be also."
(Matthew 6:21)

"For the wages of sin is death, but the gift of God is eternal life in Christ Jesus our Lord."
(Romans 6:23)

"Commit to the Lord whatever you do, and he will establish your plans."
(Proverbs 16:3)

"Jabez cried out to the God of Israel, 'Oh, that you would bless me and enlarge my territory! Let your hand be with me and keep me from harm so that I will be free from pain.' And God granted his request."

(1 Chronicles 4:10)

"But the Lord is with me like a mighty warrior, so my persecutors will stumble and not prevail. They will fail and be thoroughly disgraced; their dishonor will never be forgotten."

(Jeremiah 20:11)

"May the God who gives endurance and encouragement give you the same attitude of mind toward each other that Christ Jesus had, so that with one mind and one voice you may glorify the God and Father of our Lord Jesus Christ. Accept one another, then, just as Christ accepted you, in order to bring praise to God."

(Romans 15:5-7)

"Be strong and courageous. Do not be afraid or terrified because of them, for the Lord your God goes with you; he will never leave you nor forsake you."

(Deuteronomy 31:6)

"Do not be anxious about anything, but in every situation, by prayer and petition, with thanksgiving, present your requests to God. And the peace of God, which transcends all understanding, will guard your hearts and your minds in Christ Jesus."

(Philippians 4:6-7)

"'For I know the plans I have for you,' declares the Lord, 'plans to prosper you and not to harm you, plans to give you hope and a future.'"

(Jeremiah 29:11)

"When the Lord restored the fortunes of Zion, we were like those who dreamed. Our mouths were filled with laughter, our tongues with songs of joy. Then it was said among the nations. The Lord has done great things for them."

(Psalm 126:1-2)

"The earth is the Lord's, and everything in it, the world, and all who live in it."

(Psalm 24:1)

"Nor will people say, 'Here it is,' or 'There it is,' because the kingdom of God is in your midst."

(Luke 17:21)

"Because of the Lord's great love, we are not consumed, for his compassions never fail. They are new every morning; great is your faithfulness. I say to myself, 'The Lord is my portion; therefore, I will wait for him. The Lord is good to those whose hope is in him, to the one who seeks him.'"
(Lamentations 3:22-25)

"The name of the Lord is a fortified tower; the righteous run to it and are safe."
(Proverbs 18:10)

"For it is written: He will command his angels concerning you to guard you carefully; they will lift you up in their hands so that you will not strike your foot against a stone."
(Luke 4:10-11)

"I can do all this through him who gives me strength."
(Philippians 4:13)

"The angel of the Lord encamps around those who fear him, and he delivers them."
(Psalm 34:7)

"Trust in the Lord with all your heart and lean not on your own understanding; in all your ways submit to him, and he will make your paths straight."

(Proverbs 3:5-6)

"The thief comes only to steal and kill and destroy; I have come that they may have life and have it to the full."

(John 10:10)

"I called to the Lord, who is worthy of praise, and I have been saved from my enemies."

(Psalm 18:3)

"So do not fear, for I am with you; do not be dismayed, for I am your God. I will strengthen you and help you; I will uphold you with my righteous right hand."

(Isaiah 41:10)

"But when you ask, you must believe and not doubt because the one who doubts is like a wave of the sea, blown and tossed by the wind."

(James 1:6)

"Some trust in chariots and some in horses, but we trust in the name of the Lord our God."

(Psalm 20:7)

"Though he slay me, yet will I hope in him; I will surely defend my ways to his face."
(Job 13:15)

"Do not be overcome by evil but overcome evil with good."
(Romans 12:21)

"Look to the Lord and his strength; seek his face always."
(1 Chronicles 16:11)

"The grass withers and the flowers fall, but the word of our God endures forever."
(Isaiah 40:8)

"However, the Lord your God would not listen to Balaam but turned the curse into a blessing for you because the Lord your God loves you."
(Deuteronomy 23:5)

"And we know that in all things God works for the good of those who love him, who have been called according to his purpose."
(Romans 8:28)

"Listen to my prayer, O God, do not ignore my plea."
(Psalm 55:1)

"Lord, hear my voice. Let your ears be attentive to my cry for mercy."
(Psalm 130:2)

"Jesus looked at them and said, 'With man this is impossible, but with God all things are possible.'"
(Matthew 19:26)

"My heart says of you, 'Seek his face!' Your face, Lord, I will seek."
(Psalm 27:8)

"By day, the Lord directs his love, at night his song is with me— a prayer to the God of my life."
(Psalm 42:8).

"And the God of all grace, who called you to his eternal glory in Christ, after you have suffered a little while, will himself restore you and make you strong, firm and steadfast."
(1 Peter 5:10)

Scriptures for Daily Prayer

Scriptures for Daily Prayer

_____

_____

_____

_____

_____

_____

_____

_____

_____

_____

_____

_____

_____

_____

_____

_____

_____

_____

_____

_____

_____

_____

_____

_____

Scriptures for Daily Prayer

Scriptures for Daily Prayer

Scriptures for Daily Prayer

Scriptures of Reflection

Scriptures of Reflection

Scriptures of Reflection

Scriptures of Reflection

Scriptures of Reflection

Scriptures of Victory

Scriptures of Victory

Scriptures of Victory

_____

_____

_____

_____

_____

_____

_____

_____

_____

_____

_____

_____

_____

_____

_____

_____

_____

_____

_____

_____

_____

_____

_____

Scriptures of Victory

Scriptures of Victory

My Reign Reflections and Revelations in Prayer

The following pages are for your journey. Utilize this space to initiate your prayers and jot down your favorite Scriptures. When you write what is on your heart, it helps you process what you feel and see where you need to focus your prayers. Consider sharing how you feel, writing a prayer, or penning a Scripture that correlates to your feelings and thoughts.

Today, I will resolve what I feel by writing it…

I will release it to God in prayer…

I will be restored through Scripture…

Today, I will resolve what I feel by writing it...

_____

_____

_____

_____

_____

_____

_____

_____

I will release it to God in prayer...

_____

_____

_____

_____

_____

_____

_____

_____

I will be restored through Scripture…

_____

_____

_____

_____

_____

_____

_____

_____

_____

"God is spirit, and his worshipers must worship in the Spirit and in truth." (John 4:24)

Today, I will resolve what I feel by writing it...

_____

_____

_____

_____

_____

_____

_____

_____

_____

I will release it to God in prayer...

_____

_____

_____

_____

_____

_____

_____

_____

_____

I will be restored through Scripture...

_____

_____

_____

_____

_____

_____

_____

_____

_____

**"My comfort in my suffering is this: Your promise preserves
my life." (Psalm 119:50)**

Today, I will resolve what I feel by writing it…

_____

_____

_____

_____

_____

_____

_____

_____

I will release it to God in prayer…

_____

_____

_____

_____

_____

_____

_____

_____

I will be restored through Scripture…

_____

_____

_____

_____

_____

_____

_____

_____

_____

"Look to the Lord and his strength; seek his face always."
(1 Chronicles 16:11)

Today, I will resolve what I feel by writing it…

_____

_____

_____

_____

_____

_____

_____

_____

I will release it to God in prayer…

_____

_____

_____

_____

_____

_____

_____

_____

I will be restored through Scripture…

_____

_____

_____

_____

_____

_____

_____

_____

_____

**God, today, I believe You to make crooked places
straight, old things new, and the impossible possible. In
Jesus' name, Amen.**

Today, I will resolve what I feel by writing it...

_____

_____

_____

_____

_____

_____

_____

_____

I will release it to God in prayer...

_____

_____

_____

_____

_____

_____

_____

_____

I will be restored through Scripture...

_____

_____

_____

_____

_____

_____

_____

_____

_____

"The grass withers and the flowers fall, but the word of our God endures forever." (Isaiah 40:8)

Today, I will resolve what I feel by writing it...

_____

_____

_____

_____

_____

_____

_____

_____

I will release it to God in prayer...

_____

_____

_____

_____

_____

_____

_____

_____

I will be restored through Scripture…

_____

_____

_____

_____

_____

_____

_____

_____

_____

"The name of the Lord is a fortified tower; the righteous run to it and are safe." (Proverbs 18:10)

Today, I will resolve what I feel by writing it...

_____

_____

_____

_____

_____

_____

_____

_____

I will release it to God in prayer...

_____

_____

_____

_____

_____

_____

_____

_____

I will be restored through Scripture...

_____

_____

_____

_____

_____

_____

_____

_____

_____

God, I thank You for the power of prayer that reveals itself in private for what You will do publicly. In Jesus' name, Amen.

Today, I will resolve what I feel by writing it...

_____

_____

_____

_____

_____

_____

_____

_____

I will release it to God in prayer...

_____

_____

_____

_____

_____

_____

_____

_____

I will be restored through Scripture…

_____

_____

_____

_____

_____

_____

_____

_____

_____

**Today, I declare that God remembers and answers my
prayers from long ago. In Jesus' name, Amen.**

Prayer Request

Prayer Request

_____
_____
_____
_____
_____
_____

_____
_____
_____
_____
_____
_____

_____
_____
_____
_____
_____

Prayer Request

Prayer Request

_____
_____
_____
_____
_____
_____

_____
_____
_____
_____
_____
_____

_____
_____
_____
_____
_____

Prayers God has Answered

Prayers God has Answered

Prayers God has Answered

Prayers God has Answered

_____

_____

_____

_____

_____

_____

_____

_____

_____

_____

_____

_____

_____

_____

_____

_____

_____

About The Author

Toni Roberts Sinegal is a daughter of the King, wife, mother, passionate minister of the Gospel, spiritual midwife, and example of God using the least likely to raise them up and reflect His glory in the Earth. Toni has an unwavering belief that once we surrender, God can build beautiful things from our broken places. Toni has a heart for the healing, development, and the special purpose of women everywhere, demonstrating Christ through servant leadership through daily prayer, intercession, empowerment, Biblical truth, and speaking engagements. Although short in stature, she stands tall in God's grace. Through her ministry, Toni's greatest aspiration is to be emptied every time she encounters those God has assigned her to pour into. Toni understands that our story and scars can be used to point others to Christ for the glory of God and firmly believes that the root of success is birthed in the private and intimate place of prayer. Toni is devoted to the strategies, power, and fruit of prayer through a relationship with God and His holy Word.

Let's Stay Connected!

 @ToniRobertsSinegal

 @Toni_Sinegal

 info@ToniRobertsSinegal.com

 www.tonirobertssinegal.com

Made in the USA
Columbia, SC
09 October 2021

46650475R00059